P9-DEI-171

# APOLLO & DAPHNE

## MASTERPIECES OF GREEK MYTHOLOGY

RETOLD BY ANTONIA BARBER

WITH PAINTINGS FROM THE GREAT ART MUSEUMS OF THE WORLD

THE J. PAUL GETTY MUSEUM
LOS ANGELES

**For my sister Pamela Oldfield,
with love and thanks**

At The J. Paul Getty Museum:

Christopher Hudson, Publisher; Mark Greenberg,
Managing Editor; John Harris, Shelly Kale, Editors

First published in the United States in 1998 by
The J. Paul Getty Museum, 1200 Getty Center Drive,
Suite 1000, Los Angeles, California 90049-1687

Apollo & Daphne was first edited, produced, and published in 1998 by Frances
Lincoln Limited, 4 Torriano Mews, Torriano Avenue, London NW5 2RZ

PHOTOGRAPHIC ACKNOWLEDGMENTS
For permission to reproduce the paintings on the following pages
and/or supplying photographs, the publishers thank:
The J. Paul Getty Museum, Los Angeles: 11, 18, Back Cover
Kunsthistorisches Museum, Vienna: 35
Louvre, Paris/Giraudon/Bridgeman Art Library, London: 17
Photograph © 1992 The Metropolitan Museum of Art: 29
The National Gallery, London: Front Cover, 13, 21, 32, 37, 38, 41
© 1997 Board of Trustees, National Gallery of Art, Washington: 8
Scala, Florence: 4, 14, 22, 31
Southampton City Art Gallery/Bridgeman Art Library, London: 25, 26

**Library of Congress Cataloging-in-Publication Data**
Barber, Antonia, 1932-
Apollo & Daphne : masterpieces of Greek mythology / retold by
Antonia Barber.
p.   cm.
Includes indexes.
ISBN 0-89236-504-8
1.Mythology, Greek, in art.   2. Painting-Themes, motives.
I Title.  II. Title:  Apollo and Daphne.
ND1420.B37   1998
753' .7--DC21        97-42834
CIP
Designed by David Fordham

Set in Goudy Old Style by MATS, Southend-on-Sea

Printed in Hong Kong
135798642

# Contents

# APOLLO & DAPHNE

THE GREAT GOD APOLLO once fell foul of Cupid, the son of Venus. Returning from the hunt, he passed the boy god playing with his tiny arrows and laughed at him, saying: "Put away your toys, little boy, lest you hurt yourself."

"See how you like the sting of my toys," muttered Cupid angrily, and taking a gold-tipped arrow of love, he fired it at the back of the departing god. Apollo did not even heed the wound, but, chancing upon the water nymph Daphne, he at once fell hopelessly in love with her. "Now, my lord, you shall feel the pain," breathed Cupid. He took a second arrow, tipped with lead, and loosed it at the beautiful nymph. Struck in the shoulder, she was not hurt but at once looked upon Apollo with loathing. For Cupid has the power to make love or destroy it.

The nymph fled from Apollo, and the god pursued her. Down the valley they went, while Cupid smiled and watched them go. "You will think twice, my lord," he said, "before you mock me again."

Apollo's plight was sad indeed. Everything about the nymph—her flowing hair, her frightened eyes, her slender form—filled him with a hopeless longing. He called out to her, offering his love and all his godly powers to please her. But poor Daphne was filled with terror at the sight of him, handsome and splendid though he was. Apollo feared that she would fall and injure herself as she fled,

and yet he could not give up the chase. Little by little he gained upon her, for his strength was great and hers was failing.

Scratched by branches, her feet bruised by stones, Daphne began to gasp for breath. She made for the deep river, hoping that her father, the river god, would save her. But Apollo's hand was on her arm. "Father!" she cried out in her despair. "Great god of the river, save me from my fate!"

Poseidon heard her cry. As she stretched out her arm, she felt it stiffen; her fingers lengthened and grew brown; green leaves sprouted from her fingertips. Her slender body became clothed in rough bark; her white feet darkened and buried themselves in the rich earth. When, at last, Apollo clasped his beloved, he found within the circle of his arms only a graceful, swaying laurel tree.

The great god wept, laying his wet cheek against the slender trunk. And Daphne took pity upon him, for the green leaves reached down and gently brushed against his face.

Then said Apollo: "Though you may never be my love, yet shall you be my sacred tree. Your leaves shall be forever green, and all men shall do you honor."

And so it is that, to this day, when men and women do noble deeds, we crown them with the green laurel that the god Apollo loved.

# VENUS & ADONIS

VENUS WAS THE GODDESS OF LOVE; she was also the goddess of spring, the season of love. She held sway over all growing things, gardens and woodlands, trees and flowers. She was mother to the boy god of love, Cupid, and yet even she was not safe from his powers.

Once, as she played with her son, she pricked her finger on one of his arrows. She paid little heed to the wound. But before it had healed, she chanced to meet the handsome Adonis as he hunted with his hounds in the forest. At once the great goddess fell hopelessly in love with the mortal man.

She followed Adonis wherever he went, constantly begging him to take care. She ordered him to hunt only hares and deer, and other animals that could not harm him. She forbade him ever to hunt lions or bears or the fierce wild boar.

Adonis pretended to obey her commands, but he was a bold young man, and he thought it beneath him to hunt only for easy prey. So when Venus went away for a while, crossing the heavens in her chariot with white swans, Adonis took up his spear. Calling to his hounds, the hunter went out to seek a more dangerous challenge.

His hounds cornered an old boar, a huge creature with fearsome tusks. Adonis threw his spear and hit the beast, but his aim was not quite true, and the blow did not strike home. Enraged, the great animal shook loose the spear, rushed at its tormentor, and buried its tusks deep in his side.

Adonis gave a great cry of pain. It rose high in the heavens and reached Venus in her winged chariot, striking her like a blow to the heart. Turning her white swans about, she drove with all speed to where her beloved mortal lay. She found him bleeding out his life upon the green grass of a forest glade, and, gathering him into her arms, the goddess wept in her despair.

Yet, for all her tears, she could not save him; she could only watch as Adonis died. Her falling tears mingled with his flowing blood. They grew, they put out leaves, and each one opened into a delicate crimson flower.

And so it is, even to this day, when spring comes in that land and the bright red windflower, the anemone, blooms over field and woodland, then people say that the great goddess Venus weeps again for her lost Adonis.

# BACCHUS & ARIADNE

BACCHUS WAS BORN OF A MORTAL WOMAN, but his father was great Jupiter. The king of gods doted upon the boy: he wished for his son a life of endless happiness. So, while Bacchus was still a youth, Jupiter made him the god of wine and revelry. He gave him old Silenus as his teacher and a band of nymphs and satyrs for his companions. They roamed the world, teaching mortals to make wine and to sing and dance. But even the gods cannot shield those they love from sorrow.

After each journey, Bacchus returned to Naxos, his favourite island, and here, one day, he found a beautiful maiden lying asleep on the shore. This was Ariadne, daughter of King Minos of Crete. Hers was a sad story: she had rescued her lover Theseus from her father's labyrinth and fled with him in search of his homeland. They had sheltered for a while on Naxos and Ariadne had fallen asleep beside her lover. But while she slept, the faithless Theseus rose up and sailed away, leaving her on the shore, where Bacchus now found her.

The young god of wine was new to love and his heart was moved by the sight of the sleeping maiden. But when Ariadne awoke to find Theseus had abandoned her, she ran wild with grief.

Now Bacchus was kind: he was a god in whom there was no envy, no cruelty. He set about comforting the wretched Ariadne, giving her wine to warm her heart and playing music to raise her spirits. Poor Ariadne had never known such care. In loving the faithless Theseus, she had given all and gained nothing. Who can wonder that Bacchus soon won her heart and that she consented to be his bride? To mark their union, the joyful god gave her a golden crown starred with seven priceless diamonds.

But their happiness was short-lived. No sooner were they wedded, than Ariadne fell sick and died. Bacchus was heartbroken. He blamed his father for not saving his beloved, and he flung her crown high up into the face of the gods.

Then the world became a wretched place. While Bacchus mourned, there was no wine, no music, no revelry in all the earth. Everywhere men prayed to the gods and they in turn implored great Jupiter to restore to Bacchus his much-loved bride. And the king of the gods, to see his son smile again, restored the lovely Ariadne to her grateful husband. Joy returned to the earth and echoed back from the heavens above, where gleamed the seven bright stars known to this day as Ariadne's crown.

# ARACHNE

THERE ONCE LIVED A YOUNG WOMAN named Arachne who took great pride in her fine weaving. Her cloth was much admired, and word of it reached Athene (Athena, goddess of war and wisdom), who was famed for that same skill. The jealous Athene disguised herself as an old woman and went to look upon her rival's handiwork.

She found Arachne surrounded by admirers. How graceful she looked, weaving her shuttle back and forth across the warp threads of her loom!

"Remarkable," croaked the goddess. "Such skill! Surely the great Athene herself must have taught you!"

"Not she!" said Arachne scornfully. "I taught myself, though I weave as well as any goddess."

"Do you indeed?" replied Athene angrily, and revealed herself in her divine form.

The astonished onlookers bowed before her, but Arachne tossed her head proudly and went on weaving.

"Set up the other loom," ordered the goddess. "Then we shall see who has the greater skill."

Now Athene was cunning: into her cloth she wove pictures showing the terrible fates of mortals who defied the gods. These, she thought, would make the girl's hand tremble and so spoil her web. But when Arachne saw the pictures, she only smiled. When the task was done, the onlookers gathered around the work of the goddess, declaring it to be perfection.

Rising in triumph, Athene crossed the floor to see Arachne's loom. Then the face of Athene turned pale. Not only was the work flawless, but the girl had woven into it pictures showing the misdeeds of the gods. Arachne sat beside it, a faint smile still about her lips.

The anger of Athene was terrible to behold: ripping the cloth from her loom, she tore apart the shameful pictures. "For this insult," she breathed, "I will destroy you, as I have destroyed your work."

"Rather will I die by my own hand!" cried Arachne boldly, and, springing up onto the loom, she wound the warp threads about her neck and leapt to her death. But mortals cannot so easily escape the power of the gods. Even as Arachne fell, Athene stretched out her hand.

At her touch, the graceful body was transformed into a huge black spider, hanging from a vast web that filled the dark spaces of the roof above them. With cries of horror, those who had come to marvel now fled in fear.

"For your great skills," said the goddess, "you shall forever weave webs of beauty. But for your great pride, you yourself shall be a thing of loathing. And may such be the fate of all those who treat the gods with scorn!"

# Diana & Actaeon

Actaeon was a hunter, a young man whose life was devoted to the thrill of the chase. He had a fine pack of hounds and his greatest joy was to pursue some noble stag over hill and valley, until at last the great beast tired and the clamoring hounds pulled it down.

He was a strong and tireless runner who often outstripped his friends and fellow huntsmen. So it chanced one afternoon that he found himself alone in a deep valley. The stag had taken to the river, covering its scent and leaving the hounds in confusion. Actaeon was hot, and he remembered a pool below a waterfall where he could drink and bathe.

As he drew near the pool, he heard silvery laughter amid the splashing water. He paused and smiled, guessing that water nymphs had found his bathing place. But instead of turning modestly away, the young man crept closer. He parted the bushes to spy on the naked nymphs.

What he saw made him gasp: rising head and shoulders above the laughing nymphs, with the moon crescent gleaming in her hair, stood the great Diana, goddess of the hunt. And as he gazed upon her naked figure, the goddess turned her head and saw him.

Actaeon's blood ran cold: he knew that such sights are forbidden to mortal men, and he knew that his fate would be terrible. Diana's stare transfixed him. Since she had no arrows at hand, she raised her strong arm and sent flying a shower of water droplets. They arched through the sunlit air and struck Actaeon across the face.

The hunter turned and fled, but it was too late. A strange shudder ran through his body. His legs grew thin, and his feet shrank and hardened into hoofs. Fur covered his skin, and wide antlers sprouted from his forehead. He found himself running swiftly on four legs, and for a moment he was glad of the speed it gave him. Then he heard the baying of hounds and saw in the distance his own pack, which had caught his scent and now came pouring over the mountainside like quicksilver.

His plight was desperate. His stag's heart pounded, his strong muscles ached. On and on he ran, mile after mile, while the voices of his friends shouted encouragement to the hounds.

At last he stumbled, and at once the hounds were upon him, tearing at his flesh. The huntsmen surrounded him as he fell to the ground. He could hear them lamenting that their good friend Actaeon had missed the kill; then he sank into the merciful silence of death.

# EUROPA & THE BULL

JUPITER, THE KING OF THE GODS, once fell in love with a princess named Europa. She was the daughter of the king of Phoenicia and was very beautiful. The great god watched her with longing as she played in the fields with her maidens. But he knew that Juno, his queen, would destroy any mortal who shared her husband's love.

There were cattle grazing in the fields that stretched along the margin of the sea, so Jupiter turned himself into a fiery white bull and joined the other cattle near the spot where Europa was playing. He approached the maiden gently and lowered his great horned head as if to play with her.

Europa was enchanted by the friendly beast. She made a garland for his neck. Then, when he knelt before her, she climbed up onto his broad back. Holding fast to his horns, she rode about, laughing, while her attendants called to her, warning her to take care. But no sooner was she in his power than the white bull ran down to the seashore and plunged into the waves. Europa screamed and her maidens cried out, but the bull swam on out to sea. Waves broke over them; Europa was very wet and very frightened.

Then, to her astonishment, the white bull spoke. He confessed to her that he was, in truth, the god Jupiter.

He declared his great love and told how he had disguised himself to save her from the wrath of Juno.

Europa listened and grew calm. She felt flattered that the king of the gods should humble himself for love of her beauty.

At last they reached the island of Crete. Here Jupiter resumed his godlike form and hid Europa in a grove of willows, where he could visit her in secret. For many years the god remained her lover, and in the course of time she bore him three fine sons. Jupiter kept them all hidden from the eyes of Juno, but as they grew up, he knew that they must be prepared for the world of men.

Now, it happened that the king of Crete was old and childless. When Jupiter brought to his notice the lovely Europa and her three handsome boys, the lonely king longed to make them his own. He asked Europa to marry him and, with Jupiter's blessing, she consented. So Europa became queen of Crete and her devoted husband adopted the three sons of Jupiter. The eldest boy, Minos, took his place as heir to the throne, and after the death of the old king, he became the most famous of all the kings of Crete.

# ECHO & NARCISSUS

JUNO, THE QUEEN OF THE GODS, had among her many attendants a lovely wood nymph named Echo. Juno was very fond of her, but, unfortunately, the little nymph talked too much, and Juno grew tired of the sound of her voice. What was worse, Echo always tried to have the last word, which was not only disrespectful to the queen of the gods, but also very irritating.

One day, Juno could bear it no longer. "You shall have the last word," she told Echo angrily. "But you shall have no other. And the last word you have shall not be your own." From that moment, Echo was unable to speak unless she repeated words already spoken.

The poor nymph pined until she became a thin shadow. She left her companions and roamed the lonely valleys, where her faint voice could sometimes be heard repeating the calls of happier mortals.

One day, as she wandered, she came upon Narcissus, a young boy on the brink of manhood. So beautiful was this youth that all women loved him, and Echo was no exception. She longed to speak her love but could not; she could only wait for his words.

Hearing her footstep, Narcissus called out, "Who is here?" "Here! . . . here!" answered Echo, stepping forward and reaching out her arms to him. Narcissus drew back.

"No! Do not touch me!" he said. "Touch me! . . . touch me!" pleaded Echo, and she grasped his hand. Narcissus frowned and pulled his hand away. "Never can I love you!" he told her coldly. "I love you! . . . I love you!" cried Echo desperately, but Narcissus would not heed her.

Echo thought him cruel and heartless. She prayed to Juno that he too might love without return. And the goddess heard her.

As Narcissus turned away from Echo, he caught sight of a most beautiful face in a pool nearby. Enchanted, he leaned over the pool, tracing each line of the adorable features, and, for the first time, he fell in love. But the face he saw was his own, and when he reached to embrace it, his fingers met only the coldness of water. Narcissus wept, but his falling tears only blurred the image.

Then the unhappy youth began to pine, as Echo had pined for him. Unable to tear himself away from the vision of his own face, he grew thin and faded. "Alas!" he murmured, "I shall die of my love." And poor Echo replied, "My love! . . . my love!"

Narcissus died beside the pool, but Venus, goddess of love and of flowers, took pity on the lovely boy. Where he had lain, a new flower sprang up, a flower with white and golden petals, which to this day we call the narcissus.

# ACIS & GALATEA

GALATEA WAS A SEA NYMPH who fell in love with a young shepherd named Acis. His father was Faunus and his mother a sea nymph, and he was as handsome as Galatea was beautiful. But their love was doomed from the start.

Long before they met, Galatea had unwittingly won the heart of the one-eyed giant Polyphemus. He was grazing his sheep by the shore when the nymph passed by with her sea companions in a chariot drawn by dolphins. Now, Polyphemus was a Cyclops, a race that cannot stand the water, so he could not pursue her. But he waited until she came ashore and then approached her with offers of marriage.

Galatea was horrified. Not only was he huge—so large that he used a pine tree for a staff—but he was very ugly. He was dirty, too, and unkempt: his fear of water meant that he never washed, and he smelled dreadful. Galatea did not spare his feelings. She told him that she found him repulsive, and she told him why.

Polyphemus was downcast, but he did not despair. He trimmed his hair with a scythe and combed it with a hay rake. He rolled in scented flowers to improve his smell—and devastated an entire valley. Then he presented himself to Galatea again, telling her of the wealth of his flocks and offering her a life of plenty.

The sea nymph was not impressed. She told him that if he were the last man on earth, she would prefer to die a maid.

Polyphemus grew angry. He lay in wait, watching for her to come ashore. But Galatea was cautious: she always waited until the giant was sleeping before she left the safety of the waters.

Then she met the shepherd Acis. She could not resist the blue eyes and curling locks of the handsome boy. Galatea fell deeply in love, and her love made her reckless.

Polyphemus woke one day as she tiptoed past him, and he saw in her face that she loved another. He followed her up the valley, and, climbing onto a rocky promontory, he was horrified to look down and behold his beloved in the arms of the young shepherd. With a cry of rage, the giant pushed a great rock down upon the unsuspecting lovers.

As it hurtled toward them, Galatea leapt into the stream nearby, but Acis was crushed beneath the weight of the stone. His groans were terrible, and Galatea cried out to the gods to help him.

Her cry was heard: the blood that flowed from beneath the stone turned pale, then clear, and burst forth in a gushing stream. The river, which had once been her lover, now embraced Galatea and flowed caressingly about her, as she swam back to the sea that was her home.

# PERSEUS

THE KING OF ARGOS had a daughter named Danaë. He loved her dearly until, one day, he learned from the oracle that he was doomed to die at the hand of his own grandson. The king was horrified. To escape his fate, he locked up his daughter in a high tower where no man would ever see her.

But nothing is hidden from the gods. Great Jupiter saw Danaë's beauty and fell in love with her. He decided to visit her, and disguised himself as a shower of gold, because he feared the wrath of his wife Juno. Danaë was enchanted as the gold glittered about her and astonished when the god resumed his own form. She could not resist his charms. Jupiter became her lover, and she bore him a fine son, whom she named Perseus.

When the king learned of his grandson's birth, he was terrified. But he shrank from slaying one of his own blood. Instead, he shut mother and son in an old chest and set them adrift on the sea. But Jupiter did not abandon Danaë. He brought the chest safely ashore on the island of Seriphus, where they were rescued by a fisherman. This honest man took them to the court of the king, who was his brother, and there Danaë raised her son to manhood. She was still very beautiful, and in time the king sought to marry her; but Danaë had eyes only for her son. The king grew jealous and mocked the young man, calling him a "mother's boy." He challenged Perseus to prove his manhood and sent him on a quest to slay Medusa, a monstrous Gorgon with serpents for hair and a face so hideous that all who looked upon her were turned to stone.

Perseus rashly accepted the challenge. When Jupiter heard of it, he called upon the goddess Athene, who was the sworn enemy of Medusa. Athene appeared to Perseus and lent him her famous shield, warning him never to look directly at the Gorgon, only at her reflection in the shield's polished surface. Then she sent Perseus to seek out the nymphs of the Hesperides. They also gave him powerful gifts: winged sandals, a helmet that made its wearer invisible, and a black bag in which to carry safely the Gorgon's head.

With the help of these treasures, Perseus eventually found Medusa and, gazing into his shining shield, swooped down and struck off her head. Keeping his eyes tightly closed, he felt for the hideous trophy and tied it securely inside the black bag.

As he was flying back toward Seriphus, he saw below him a beautiful maiden chained to a rock and about to be devoured by a fearsome sea monster. At once Perseus attacked the foul creature with his sword. The serpent writhed and lashed its scaly tail, but the wound was mortal, and at last it sank beneath the waves.

Perseus freed the maiden, who told him that she was Andromeda, a king's daughter, and that she had been

sacrificed to free her father's land from the ravages of the monster. Perseus took her back to her parents, who welcomed them with great rejoicing. The hero told them of his adventures, and Andromeda asked to see the fearsome head. Perseus warned her of its power and let her glimpse it reflected in a pool of water. The princess's heart was won by the handsome youth, and she agreed to be his bride.

But Andromeda had earlier been promised to another suitor. On their wedding day, he appeared with a band of armed men, determined to kill his rival and reclaim his bride. Perseus was unarmed, but he reacted swiftly. Calling upon his friends to look away, he took out Medusa's head from its bag and held it aloft, and at once his attackers were turned to figures of stone!

After their marriage, Perseus took Andromeda back to Seriphus, where they found that the king had cruelly imprisoned Danaë because she still refused to marry him. Once again, Perseus took out the Gorgon's head, and the tyrant was turned to stone. He freed his mother, who advised him to give the throne to the king's brother, the honest fisherman. Then Perseus gave back to Athene the gifts of the gods and asked her to take charge of the fearsome head. This the goddess did—and placed the head of her old enemy in the center of her famous shield.

Danaë longed for her homeland. Word had reached her that her father had been imprisoned by a usurper, and, in spite of the wrong he had done them, she begged her son to take her back to Argos. There, Perseus soon overcame the false king and restored his grandfather to his rightful throne.

When the old king saw how honorably his grandson treated him, he bitterly regretted his former cruelty. He lost his fear of Perseus and decided that the oracle must have been mistaken.

But, one summer, as the king was watching his grandson at sport, Perseus threw a discus that accidentally struck the old man and killed him instantly. Then it became clear to all men that the oracle of the gods spoke truly and no man could escape the fate that lay in store for him.

# ORION

ORION WAS A GIANT renowned through all the world for his beauty and for his skill at hunting. His days were spent in pursuit of wild animals with his great dog Sirius at his heels.

One day, while he was hunting in the island of Chios, he fell in love with the king's daughter Merope. The king did not want Orion for a son-in-law, but he was afraid to refuse the giant. So he promised that he would give his daughter to Orion only if he cleared the whole island of savage beasts. The king thought this would be impossible, but Orion killed every one and piled the dead animals in a great heap before the palace doors. The king then tried to avoid his promise: he asked for proof that not a single beast remained. Orion grew angry and tried to steal Merope by force, but the king prevented him and, after drugging the giant with wine, put out his eyes.

Orion was wretched: he could no longer hunt, and his beauty was destroyed. In despair, he consulted the oracle and was told that he could regain his sight only by gazing at the sun god Helios as he rose out of the eastern ocean. Orion found a boat and rowed out to sea. But he could not tell which way he was going and was soon helplessly adrift.

At last he heard the sound of a hammer in the distance. He rowed toward the steady blows and came to the island of Lemnos, where Vulcan had his forge. The smith god took pity on blind Orion and lifted his apprentice Cedalion up onto the giant's shoulders to guide him. Together they traveled until they came to the eastern coast, where the rising sun healed Orion's sight and restored his beauty.

One day, out hunting again, Orion met with the great goddess Diana. She was so impressed by his skill and so delighted by his beauty that she decided to marry him. But this displeased her brother Apollo, who felt it would degrade his sister to wed a mere mortal. One day, when Orion was swimming far out at sea, Apollo challenged his sister to shoot an arrow at a dark speck on the horizon. Diana, never suspecting that it was her lover, took aim, and her arrow struck Orion in the head.

When the giant's body was washed ashore, the goddess wept to see what she had done. To mark her sorrow, she placed Orion among the stars, where he still strides the heavens with his belt and his bow and his faithful dog Sirius at his heels.

# DAEDALUS & ICARUS

DAEDALUS WAS AN INVENTOR, a man of great skill and cunning, who built the great Labyrinth for King Minos of Crete. But when it was finished, the king was troubled to think that Daedalus knew all its secrets, and he imprisoned him with his young son Icarus in a lonely tower. They managed to escape, but Minos sent his men out to hunt for them. Every harbor was watched, every ship searched, to make sure that they did not leave the island.

Daedalus and Icarus hid in a cave high on the sea cliffs. As he watched the gulls soaring over the sea, the inventor saw a way to escape. "I shall make wings," he said, "and we will fly away."

He set to work fashioning a framework of strong, thin branches shaped like the wings of a bird. Covering it with gulls' feathers, he fastened the larger ones with thread and the smaller ones with wax. Then he lifted the wings and, finding that they bore his weight, flew out over the water. When he landed, he looked closely at the wings and saw that the hot sun had softened their wax. "We must fly at daybreak," he said to Icarus, "and reach land before the sun grows hot." Then he set to work and made smaller wings for his son.

At the first grey light, they leapt from the cliff top and soared out over the sea. On and on they flew, until the growing light showed them land ahead. The sun rose behind clouds, and Daedalus became anxious, afraid that it would grow hot before they reached the distant shore. He flew on ahead and found a safe landing place on the rocky cliffs. Then he took off the cumbersome wings and stretched out his arms to catch the approaching Icarus.

Just then, the sun burst through the clouds, flooding the world with light. Icarus was thrilled by the vision of the land beneath him. He soared up into the sky, marveling at the fine city and the splendid ships. He saw below him a man plowing and another tending sheep. He felt like a god, looking down from heaven upon mere mortals below. The sun blazed in the sky and the wax grew soft; the feathers began to fall around him.

Suddenly, Icarus saw his danger and heard his father calling. But even as he swooped toward his father, the wings lost their power. Daedalus watched in horror as his son fell like a stone into the sea. For a brief moment the boy's legs kicked wildly above the water, and then the father was left alone with his great burden of grief.

# ORPHEUS & EURYDICE

IT IS SAID OF ORPHEUS that he was the greatest musician the world has ever known. If so, it is no wonder, for he was the son of the muse Calliope, and his father was the great god Apollo. While he was yet a child, his father gave him his lute, and Calliope herself taught him to sing and to play.

So wonderful was the singing of Orpheus that every heart was moved by the sound. When he played his lute, savage beasts grew tame and lay down in peace beside their prey, rocks moved closer to him, and trees were seen to dance. Even the gods on high Olympus made him welcome among them. As for mortal men, when Orpheus played, he soothed their pain and calmed their anger, and they held no man in greater honor.

Small wonder, then, that his playing won the heart of the lovely nymph Eurydice, with whom he had fallen in love. Gods, men, and beasts all rejoiced at their wedding feast, and Orpheus played more beautifully than ever before. But their joy was short-lived: before the sun had set on that same day, the lovely Eurydice was dead. As she left the wedding feast with her maidens to prepare for the bridal chamber, she was bitten on the heel by a poisonous snake and died in the arms of her weeping husband.

Orpheus refused to be comforted. He cried out to great Jupiter, imploring him to restore his bride to life. The king

of the gods would willingly have granted his plea for love of his sweet music, but Eurydice was now in the power of his brother Pluto, king of the Underworld. Jupiter could only grant Orpheus permission to seek his lost bride in those dark realms forbidden to mortal men, but he warned him that no one had ever returned from Pluto's kingdom. Orpheus would not be deterred; he was determined to find his lost love and win her freedom.

Playing as he went, Orpheus made his way down into the realm of the Shades, and at the sound of his music, Charon, the ferryman of the dead, rowed him across the dark River Styx. He set Orpheus down at the very gates of the Underworld, where the three-headed dog Cerberus stood guard. A softly played tune lulled the fierce creature into sleep, and the bars of the great gates slid open of their own accord.

Orpheus entered the Underworld and passed through visions of terrifying torment. But so sad was his music that the damned wept for his suffering rather than their own. It is said that even the Fates, most dreaded by men, shed a tear as he passed by. At last he came to the throne of dark Pluto and his queen, the fair Persephone. So moved was she by his sorrow and his sad music that she persuaded her stern husband to let Eurydice go free.

But Pluto made strict conditions. He told Orpheus that he must return by the same way he had come, never ceasing to sing and to play his lyre. He promised that the shadow of Eurydice should follow in his footsteps. But he warned Orpheus that he must not look back or attempt to speak to his bride until they were both in the world of the living. If he did either, Pluto decreed that Eurydice must return once more to the Underworld.

Orpheus agreed, and he set out on the long journey back to the light. Again he passed through the infernal regions, but this time he played so happily that souls in torment felt their hearts gladden and their sufferings grow less. On he went, hour after hour, but the way was long, and he could hear no sound behind him. He began to doubt the word of the god, unsure if his beloved Eurydice did follow in his footsteps. He wondered how she would look. Would she be still his own fair bride, or would her beauty be faded, her lovely face gaunt after her stay in the Underworld? His longing to catch even a glimpse of her became too much for him, and at last he turned his head. For one brief moment he saw Eurydice, pale but as fair as ever. The next moment, she was gone.

When Orpheus saw what he had done, he cursed his own doubt and impatience. Weeping, he broke the strings of his lyre and never played again. Nor did he live long after that day, for his one remaining desire was for his own death, when he would at last return to the Underworld and to his lost love.

# MIDAS

Bacchus, the young god of wine, was very fond of his teacher, the old satyr Silenus.

One day, Silenus was found drunk in the land of King Midas. Fortunately, the king recognized the old satyr, treated him with honor, and restored him safely to the god. Bacchus was very grateful and told Midas to choose his own reward. Now, the king was a greedy man, and he foolishly asked that everything he touched might turn to gold. Bacchus thought it a strange choice but granted it nevertheless.

At first, Midas was delighted. He touched stones and flowers and marveled as they were transformed. He turned his throne and even his palace into gold. Then he ordered a great feast so that he could display his treasures. But when he tried to eat, the food turned into gold before it reached his lips, and the wine too, before he could take a sip. The foolish king saw his mistake. He began to fear that he would starve to death, and, falling to his knees, he begged Bacchus to take back his gift. The young god laughed, but did as Midas asked.

From that moment, the sight of gold made Midas shudder. Leaving his palace, he chose a simple country life. But though cured of his greed, nothing could save the king from his foolishness. He became a follower of the woodland god Pan and listened all day to the sound of his rough pipes, declaring Pan a better musician than Apollo himself. Hearing this, Pan grew proud and challenged the great god to a contest. Midas judged between them, and, although Apollo played far more sweetly, the king flatteringly proclaimed Pan the winner.

Apollo was deeply insulted. "If you can hear no better than that," he declared, "you shall have the ears you deserve." Alarmed, Midas rushed to look at his face in a nearby pool and found to his horror that he had asses' ears! Ashamed to be seen, he wound a scarf about his head to hide the long, furry ears and, for the rest of his life, wore a great turban. Only the barber who cut the king's hair knew what lay hidden beneath it, and he was sworn to secrecy.

For many years, the barber told no one, but at last the burden of his secret became too much for him. Unable to stay silent any longer, he found a lonely spot by the river bank, dug a deep hole, and whispered into it the terrible truth. Then he quickly filled in the hole and went home feeling much better. But the reeds that grew all around had caught the faint whisper, and, to this day, when the wind passes over, they repeat: "Midas has asses' ears . . . Midas has asses' ears . . !"

# HOW THE TROJAN WAR BEGAN

WHEN KING PELEUS married the lovely sea nymph Thetis, all the gods, save one, came to the wedding. Eris, goddess of discord, was not invited, lest she should spoil the happy event. But the angry goddess came, all the same, and threw into their midst a golden apple. On it was written "For the Fairest."

At once, three of the most powerful goddesses laid claim to it. Juno, queen of the gods; Athene, goddess of wisdom; and Venus, goddess of love, all asked Jupiter to judge between them who was the fairest. But Jupiter was wary and claimed that, as the husband of Juno, he could not be the judge. Instead, he sent them to Mount Ida to ask a young shepherd called Paris to choose the fairest.

Now, Paris was not the simple shepherd he appeared to be, for he was the son of King Priam of Troy. At his birth, it had been foretold that he would bring destruction upon the city, so as a baby he had been left to die upon the mountainside. Here he would have perished, had he not been found and raised by a kindly shepherd.

The goddesses found the handsome youth and each secretly offered him a rich reward if he judged her the fairest. Juno offered him power, and Athene, wisdom.

But Venus offered him the love of the most beautiful woman in the world. Paris awarded the golden apple to Venus. Then the goddess told him the secret of his birth and sent him to Troy to seek his father.

King Priam was delighted to see his lost son; but his counselors reminded him of the prophecy and advised him either to kill the youth or to banish him from the city.

Now, many years before, the sister of King Priam had been stolen away to Greece. The king gave Paris a fleet of ships, and sent him in search of her.

So Paris set sail for Greece and arrived by chance at the court of Menelaus, King of Sparta. The king presented the young Trojan to Helen, his queen, boasting that all Greece hailed her as the most beautiful woman in the world. Paris at once fell in love with the queen. Venus kept her promise, and the fair Helen returned his love. Secretly, they stole away to the Trojan ships, and the triumphant Paris returned with her to Troy.

Great was the anger of Menelaus when he discovered that they had gone. He called upon all the kings of Greece to avenge the insult and help him recover his queen. A great fleet of Greek warships was made ready and the long Trojan War began.

# THE RETURN OF ODYSSEUS

ONE OF THE GREEK KINGS WHO FOUGHT AT TROY was Odysseus of Ithaca. He went to war reluctantly, since it took him away from his wife, the fair Penelope, and his much-loved baby son Telemachus.

The war lasted many long years, and brave men perished on both sides. But Odysseus survived and, weary with fighting, set sail at last for home. However, his troubles were not over. For ten long years it was his fate to roam the seas, driven by contrary winds, losing ships and companions and surviving the most terrifying adventures.

Meanwhile, in Ithaca, Telemachus grew to manhood while Penelope remained as lovely as ever. Many suitors besieged the palace, assuring her that Odysseus was certainly long dead and clamoring for her to take a new husband. But Penelope clung to the belief that one day Odysseus would return. The suitors made her life wretched and demanded that she choose one among them. They camped in the palace, eating her stores and drinking Odysseus' fine wines. Penelope promised to make her choice as soon as she had finished her tapestry; each day she wove a little more, but each night she crept down and unraveled the day's work. Seeing so little progress, the suitors grew restless and suspicious.

The day came at last when Odysseus reached Ithaca, alone and unheralded. He found the hut of his faithful swineherd Eumaeus and learned from him of the state of affairs at the palace. He sent word to Telemachus, who met him at the hut, and father and son embraced each other with grateful tears. Then they plotted to rid themselves of the suitors.

Telemachus returned to the palace and told his mother she must give the suitors a test. Penelope took down the great bow that Odysseus had once used, and said that she would only marry the man who could bend it, string it, and fire an arrow. She asked Telemachus to judge the contest and retired to her chamber.

Meanwhile, Odysseus came into the room disguised as an old beggar.

One by one, the suitors tried to bend the bow, but without success. Then the old beggar asked to take his turn. The suitors laughed, but Telemachus said, "Let him try." With the bow in his hands, the stooping beggar raised himself to his full height. Effortlessly, he bent the bow and fastened the bowstring. His first arrow transfixed the most troublesome of the suitors, and the others lived only as long as it took to fit and fire a flight of arrows.

Then, having put his house in order, Odysseus left the hall with its dead and dying and went to seek the faithful wife who had awaited his homecoming for so many years.

# INDEX OF ARTISTS AND PAINTINGS

▲ Page 17 **Diana, the Huntress** (detail)
SCHOOL OF FONTAINEBLEAU (c.1530–1560)
Louvre, Paris
*Oil on panel, 191 x 132 cm*

▼ Page 18 / Back Cover **The Abduction of Europa** (detail)
REMBRANDT (1606–1669)
The J. Paul Getty Museum, Los Angeles
*Oil on panel, 62.2 x 77 cm*

▲ Page 21 **Narcissus** (detail)
Follower of LEONARDO (painted about 1490–1499)
The National Gallery, London
*Oil on wood, painted surface 23.2 x 26.4 cm*

▼ Page 22 **The Triumph of Galatea** (detail)
RAPHAEL (1483–1520)
Palazzo della Farnesina, Rome
*Fresco, 300 x 220 cm*

▲ Page 25 **Perseus and the Sea Nymph** (detail)
SIR EDWARD BURNE-JONES (1833–1898)
Southampton City Art Gallery
*Gouache on paper, 152.8 x 126 cm*

▼ Page 26 **The Baleful Head** (detail)
SIR EDWARD BURNE-JONES (1833–1898)
Southampton City Art Gallery
*Gouache on paper, 153.7 x 129 cm*

▲ Page 29 **Blind Orion Searching for the Rising Sun**
NICHOLAS POUSSIN (1594–1665)
The Metropolitan Museum of Art, Fletcher Fund, 1924 (24.45.1)
*Oil on canvas, 119.1 x 182.9 cm*

▼ Page 32 **Orpheus (detail)**
ROLANDT SAVERY (1576–1639)
The National Gallery, London
*Oil on oak, 53 x 81.5 cm*

▲ Page 35 **Orpheus in the Underworld (detail)**
ROLANDT SAVERY (1576–1639)
Kunsthistorisches Museum, Vienna
*Oil on wood, 27 x 35 cm*

◀ Page 31 **Landscape with the Fall of Icarus (detail)**
PIETER BRUEGEL the Elder (active 1550/1; died 1569)
Musée des Beaux Arts, Brussels
*Oil on canvas, 73.7 x 111.8 cm*

▲ Page 38 **The Abduction of Helen by Paris (detail)**
Follower of FRA ANGELICO (painted about 1450)
The National Gallery, London
*Tempera on poplar, painted surface, 29.2 x 21.6 cm*

▲ Page 41 **Penelope with the Suitors (detail)**
PINTORICCHIO (active 1481; died 1513)
The National Gallery, London
*Fresco, detached and mounted on canvas, 125.5 x 152 cm*

◀ Page 37 **The Judgement of Midas (detail)**
DOMENICHINO (1581–1641) and Assistants
The National Gallery, London
*Fresco, transferred to canvas and mounted on board, 199.4 x 89.5 cm*

# Greek/Roman Names

The Romans worshipped many of the same gods as the Greeks before them, and, in the 3rd century B.C., they decided to give those gods Roman names. In this book, we have used mainly Roman names, since they are more familiar to us from Ovid's *Metamorphoses*. However, where we feel that a particular god, such as Athene, is best known by his/her Greek name, we have used that. Here is a list of the Greek gods and their Roman equivalents:

Aphrodite, goddess of love.....................................Venus

Apollo/Helios, god of music and prophecy.............Sol

Artemis, goddess of hunting and chastity..............Diana

Athene/Athena, goddess of war and wisdom.........Minerva

Dionysus, god of wine..............................................Bacchus

Eros/Amor, god of desire........................................Cupid

Hades/Pluto, god of the Underworld......................Dis

Hephaestus, god of fire............................................Vulcan

Hera, goddess of hearth and home.........................Juno

Odysseus, hero of the Trojan War..........................Ulysses

Pan, god of flocks, forests, and pastures.................Faunus/Silvanus

Persephone/Core, goddess of the Underworld........Proserpina

Poseidon, god of seas and springs...........................Neptune

Zeus, god of the sky and father of the gods............Jupiter

# Index

# FAMILY TREE OF THE GREEK GODS

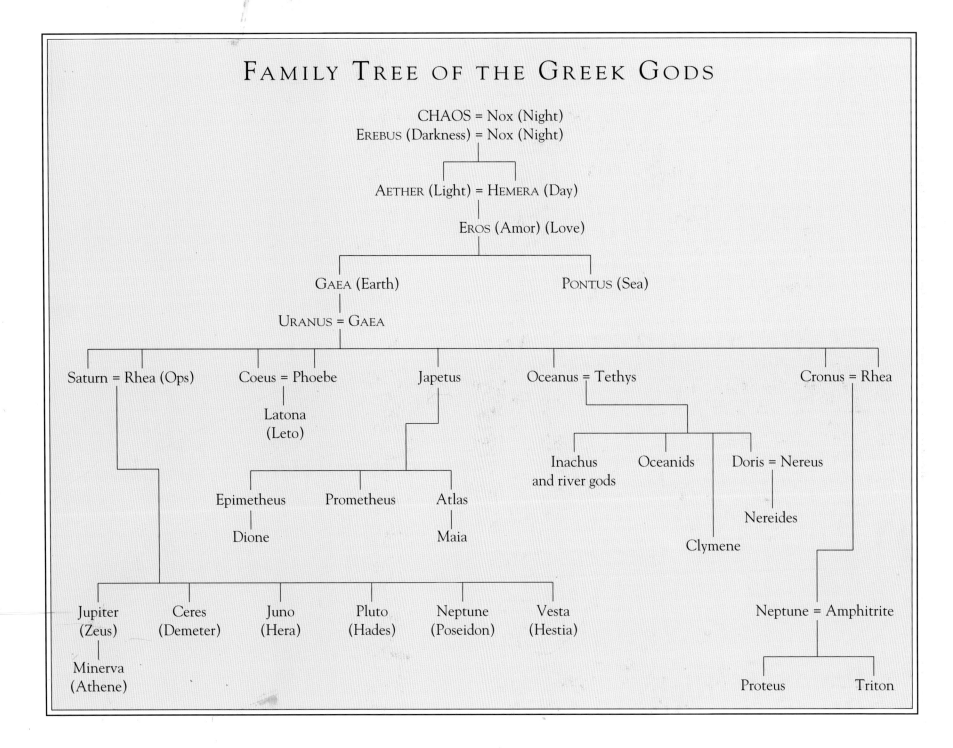